The Purposed Journey

*A Millennial and Gen-Z's Guide to Finding and Fulfilling Their
Passion and Purpose through Career or Business*

ISBN: 978-1-7348090-0-8 (Paperback)
ISBN: 978-1-7348090-1-5 (E-Book)

Library of Congress Control Number: TXu002189707

Any references to any real people are not used for monetary gain. All definitions unless notated otherwise are taken from dictionary.com.

All scriptures are taken from The Holy Bible, King James Version and New International Version.

Front cover image by Demarcus Williams, Freshdesignz, LLC. Book design by Demarcus Williams, Freshdesignz, LLC.

Printed in the United States of America.

First printing edition 2020.

Purposed2Motivate, LLC
Cary, North Carolina
Purposed2Motivate@gmail.com

www.purposed2motivate.com

THE PURPOSED JOURNEY

Table of Contents

Dedication

All the glory belongs to God. Lord, I from the bottom of
my heart, Thank You.

Ryan

Mom

Dad

Mimi

This book would not have happened without your
continuous support. I love you all.

Introduction

"Ladies and gentlemen, Ms. Kirstennnnn Williams!" The crowd went wild. I walked onto the stage, pulled the mic closer to my mouth, took a deep breath and started to sing: "Lord, I need to feel the touch of your hand." I had rehearsed Hezekiah Walker's "Second Chance" over and over again. This was my last opportunity to solidify my place in the Love Fellowship Choir.

When I was a young woman, my imagination and creativity ran wild! Not only did I perform live concerts in my room, I also drew characters that came alive in my head. Most of all, I loved doing hair. In fact, my parents have a picture of me doing my best friend's hair at the age of three. Apparently, I used grease on her European textured hair, and it didn't turn out too well. Oops!

As I got older and after a lot of practice, I began doing my own hair at the age of ten. With my parent's work schedule, it was tough for Mom to squeeze in time to do my hair, so I did my own. I was really good at it and styling my hair on my own brought me joy! My go-to style was a pony-tail to the side on the top of my head and a pony-tail at the back. As I got older, I started experimenting with wigs and extensions. Curly wigs, straight wigs, and ponytails. I had them all!

I loved being creative with my hair and changing my look any time I wanted. The ability to transform into a different person by styling my hair fascinated me! Like that time when I was 16, I wore a curly weave as a disguise to match my fake ID in order to get a navel piercing. The weave didn't work because my best friend's mom walked into the piercing shop as I was leaving and called my parents before I got home. I wish I was making this up. Needless to say, that day, I learned that hair can only transform you so much.

Anyway, while I was in high school, I began thinking about my future goals. I knew I wanted to be an entrepreneur because I had absolutely no desire to work for anyone. I loved the idea of working for myself and making my own rules. Actually, I considered myself a rebel.

I wanted to think for myself and make decisions in my life based on my own values and beliefs. I remember writing a candid letter to my parents stating that I was wild and will never be like my older brothers. I also told them frankly they would have to deal with it. As you might imagine, that didn't turn out too well, but it was my thought process at the time. Whew, child.

With that being said, entrepreneurship was perfect for me. To narrow it down even further, I knew I wanted to own a salon and day spa. At the time, this was a perfect idea. I loved doing my own hair and after researching day spas, I was hooked! My vision was so clear: "Nicole's Salon and Day Spa," named after my middle name. As you can see, the name wasn't too creative. I used my middle name because it was easier to pronounce than my first name. Hey, it worked at the time!

When I was in high school, we couldn't graduate unless we got a passing grade on our senior project. Basically, the purpose of that project was to research and study a topic that was of interest to us and then present it to a panel. I was excited about the project because I could finally share my business idea with the world.

I had everything prepared for my project: a cardboard setup of the interior and the PowerPoint presentation my dad helped me with. My dad was an executive at his company and had tons of experience with presentations and business models. He was the perfect person to assist me.

I'm a daddy's girl so working with Dad was the best! He taught me what to write in the PowerPoint and how to present it. Dad also taught me business words like "asset" and "liability." I thought I was a bad mamajama at that point. I also spent several hours researching various salons and spas as well. I had so much information on day spas I was able to create my own business plan. With my business plan, PowerPoint presentation, and design complete, I was ready to present my project to the advisory board. Here we go!

I remember as if it was yesterday. I waited in line outside the room for my turn. I could feel my heart jumping out of my chest. I was extremely nervous. Will they like my business idea? Will they like me? Will I remember the right words to say? Even though I was nervous, I was excited at the same time!

Finally, my teacher called my name: "Kirsten Williams." I took a deep breath, walked through the door and greeted the panel. I began my presentation by giving a tour of Nicole's Salon & Day Spa's floor plan while presenting my business plan on the screen. The panel was all smiles throughout my presentation and clapped for me when I finished. I thought I did an amazing job. I didn't stutter over my words, and I explained my ideas and findings thoroughly. Overall, I did my thing! Unfortunately, I was given a B on the project. Honestly, I was expecting a perfect score. However, I knew one day, they would all see me bring my vision to fruition. Entrepreneurship was my destiny. I didn't have any other career aspirations other than working for myself. I was determined to make my dreams my reality.

Chapter 1

Step 1: Be Honest with Yourself

While I was in college, I changed my major three times. I knew I wanted to become an entrepreneur; however, the business classes didn't interest me. I mean, come on, microeconomics? Really? Fail! Just kidding, that is a great class to take if you're interested in business. Just keeping it real, if I'm being totally honest, none of the classes were of any interest to me. I really did not want to be in college, but I basically had no choice. My parents *strongly* encouraged me to attend a four-year university as a backup to going to hair school.

At that time, I was rebelling because I truly wanted to be an entrepreneur, and I felt college was a waste of my time. I thought it would be so easy to obtain my cosmetologist license, find a job at a salon and then open my salon and spa by age twenty-three. Stereotypical millennial way of thinking, right? I was willing to fail my classes just so I could go home and achieve my goal.

I knew that my parents wouldn't allow me to just leave. My mom, dad, and step-mom have advanced degrees. My three older brothers went to college as well. Therefore, dropping out was not an option for me. I would've felt like the black sheep of my family, and I didn't want that. I ended my first semester with a 1.6 GPA. I failed my microeconomics class and had to withdraw from my college algebra class. I was happy and embarrassed at the same time.

Honestly, looking back, I wish I would have applied myself more and taken full advantage of my opportunity to go to college. Shortly after receiving my failing scores, I decided to get myself together.

You see, during my rebellion, I met my boyfriend Ryan, now husband, at our freshman orientation. After a couple of months into our freshman year, we started dating and our relationship was getting serious. We were inseparable and one of the well-known couples on campus. He challenged me to do better, and I did not want to go back home and leave him.

After taking one psychology class, I decided to switch my major from business to psychology. The study of the mind was so interesting to me. I also enjoyed listening to my friends' problems and giving them advice. However, once I found out that I'd have to stay in school longer to become a therapist, I switched again and finally committed to communication studies. I reconnected with my passion for writing and doing presentations.

When I was younger, I enjoyed reading, writing, and public speaking. My first speech was in 5th grade. I spoke in front of the entire school during an awards ceremony for high achievers. Little did I know that I was already operating in my calling. Fast forward to after college, I still thought I wanted to own a salon and day spa. I researched different schools and when I talked with an admissions counselor at a local community college, I realized I did not want to go in that direction any longer. I had lost my passion for doing hair. I still styled my own but when I did someone else's hair, it didn't bring me joy and fulfillment.

Now what? Owning a salon and spa was my dream. I felt lost. Shortly after deciding that the hair business wasn't for me, I had the idea to start a music academy for underprivileged children. A music academy? Random, right? Well, I have an explanation for the idea. After college, I moved to a neighboring city and met a lot of local musicians. I became very active on the music scene, so it was only a matter of time before I began to act and think like them. I started the business and incorporated it as a non-profit organization. I honestly thought the academy was going to be my big break. I just knew that my dream of owning a business by the age of twenty-three was coming to fruition. I was so wrong — extremely wrong.

I worked so hard on that business. I saved $500 and hired an attorney to file a 501(c) 3, which is tax-exempt status, and I interviewed potential board members. I was only twenty-three, but I wasn't playing any games! While working on the business, I was hired at a Fortune 500 Insurance company as a commercial processor. I was responsible for creating and making changes to commercial insurance policies. It was my first corporate job. A girl had to eat, and I was tired of being broke!

Prior to the new job, I worked at a call center, and I was over it. The angry customers, non-stop calls, and low pay were a no for me. While working as a commercial processor, I was introduced to commercial insurance claims. Once I learned that the commercial claims adjusters made at least $40,000, I was *very* interested. I was twenty-four years old by the time this position became available, so making $40K was like winning the lottery to me, especially since I was only making $27,000 at the time. After six months as a commercial processor, I interviewed for the claims position and was offered the job! Keep in mind I was still trying to get my business off the ground.

I started my new position and after work, I was grinding hard to get my business up and running. I reached out to so many people to make my dream of owning a business a reality. I almost landed a contract with a local community organization; however, a tornado hit the city and severely damaged their location. After a year of rejections and nothing seemingly going right, the business and my performance at work started to decline. I was done. I completely gave up and told myself that entrepreneurship wasn't for me anymore. I decided I was going to become a career woman and make the most out of my situation. Hey, the job was affording me the condo that I had my eyes on after moving to my new city, a newer car and several trips a year. At the time, I did not have a tremendous amount of debt, so $40K a year went a long way.

It took me four more years and lots of stress to be completely honest with myself and what I truly wanted. I made the tough decision to withdraw my 401K and resign from my corporate job of six years. Mind you, by the time I quit, my salary had increased to $65,000. That may not be much for some; however, it was a lot for me at twenty-nine years old because I knew I could be at or close to six figures by thirty-five on the path I was on. Some households with two working adults don't make that combined. So yes, $65K was a lot to me and it took a lot for me to leave.

I knew God had more for me and eventually, my income would surpass the money I left behind and what I could have potentially made. I had faith that God would make a way for me to operate in my purpose and be more fulfilled while making the money I needed and desired. A man's gift makes room for him and brings him before great men (Proverbs 18:16, KJV).

What are you not being honest about? Are you on a realistic path to fulfillment or trying to do what you see on social media? Kudos to everyone starting businesses but if I see another online boutique, I am going to scream. If you are not passionate about fashion or a cause that deals with clothing, why open a boutique? I'm tired of seeing the same clothes on one hundred different social media pages.

Follow your own path and what makes you who you are. Have you even thought about what's important to you when it comes to your career or business? How about your life? What does success and the American dream look like to you? What are you running from or running to? What drives you? These are all valid questions that will get you closer to what it is you truly want to do in a career or business.

I should have continued to work hard to achieve my goal of becoming an entrepreneur when the going got tough. I wish I had been more honest with myself years ago instead of giving up so easily. I also wish I had realized material possessions are not worth staying in a job that makes you miserable and stressed out every time you go to it. You don't have to wait until you are in your thirties to figure out your passion and purpose like I did. But even if you are older, it's not too late. You're right on time for your unique journey.

EXERCISE 1

It is very important to be honest with yourself as you work on figuring out your passion and purpose. To assist you in doing so, go to the back of this book and answer the questions in Exercise 1 with complete honesty.

Chapter 2

Step 2: Gaining Confidence Within

When I was younger, I struggled with self-confidence. I think the main reason was that I was a little chubby. I had a little bit of baby fat as most kids do; however, I grew up around skinny brothers and a slim younger sister. Also, it didn't help that my awesome and loving brothers picked on me for it. Oh, the joy of having older brothers! Anyway, the two most important women in my life, my mom and stepmom, taught me how to love myself. They would preach to me about daily self-affirmations and the love God has for us.

Once I got to middle school, I lost most of my baby weight, and I was feeling a lot better about myself. Fast-forward to my adult years, my self-confidence deteriorated again. Only this time, I lacked confidence in my God-given gifts, talents, and abilities. Quite frankly, I didn't think I had any talents or gifts. I used to say I had none because I viewed talents as something tangible. For example, if someone could play the piano beautifully or draw pictures with precision, he or she had a talent I could see or hear. However, I could not visualize what my talent was.

I would constantly hear I had a nice speaking voice. I also constantly heard that I was a great listener, motivator, and encourager. I didn't think those things were my talents. I thought it was just — me.

When people complimented me on those things, I took it at face value. I would simply thank them and keep it moving. All the while, I was still trying to figure out what I was good at. Makes no sense, right? All my life, people would tell me what my talents and gifts were, but I would ignore it to search for something that was not there.

I spent years searching for gifts that God had not blessed me with when the ones He gave me were right there all along. Why did I spend so much time searching for other gifts and talents? I did so because I was not confident in what God had already blessed me with. It took me until I was at my wit's end with my job to finally realize my natural gifts were enough to get me where I wanted to go in life.

One fall evening after work, I called my dad and stepmom for the 80th time to complain about my job and how stressed out I was. After crying about how I couldn't take it anymore, I was advised to find some quiet time and write freely in my journal about my life.

Later that night, I stopped everything I was doing and sat in silence, so I could just think about my life: what I wanted and needed. I cuddled up under my blanket on the couch and took out my journal. I began writing everything I wanted in life, as well as what I was good at and what I wasn't good at. I just let it flow out of me.

After doing that, I realized I *am* great at encouraging others. I *am* a great motivator. I *do* speak eloquently. I *am* a people person, and I love being around people. I love helping people reach their full potential, and I know how to motivate them to do so. Plus, I was darn good at all of that.

Instead of continuing my futile search for what wasn't there, I worked on what God had already blessed me with. I found the confidence I didn't have before in my own God-given abilities. I gained confidence that God would take care of and provide for me as I pursued my journey.

"And my God will meet all your needs according to the riches of his glory in Christ Jesus." - Philippians 4:19

Perhaps you are asking what self-confidence has to do with being confident in your God-given abilities and talents. Here's the answer: you must be confident in yourself before you are confident in the gifts God blessed you with. If you've been blessed with the ability to speak charismatically in front of large crowds, but you hate the way you look, it's going to reflect in your stage presence and speech.

On stage, all eyes are on you. So as a speaker, you must love the way you look. You must love the way you are. Period. No exceptions. If not, you will never get on the stage to speak. Hence, many people will miss out on what God has placed on your heart to say. If you do make it on a stage, you will be so caught up in what the crowd is thinking about you and how you look, you will stutter on your words.

Who wants to listen to a timid speaker? Nobody. People enjoy speakers who project self-confidence, not only in what they say but also in themselves. Whatever gifts and talents you have, you must be bold and confident in yourself first before you can effectively operate in them.

EXERCISE 2

By now, you may be asking how to gain confidence in yourself and your abilities. So I have written four easy steps that will boost your confidence in no time! Turn to the back of the book and complete the Four Steps to Building Your Confidence exercise.

Chapter 3

Step 3: Discovering Your Passion and Purpose

Now that you have been honest with yourself and gained confidence from within, it's time to discover what you're truly passionate about and how that aligns with your purpose.

After graduating from college, I was heavily involved in my church. I longed to know what my purpose was. I would pray constantly, asking God to reveal my purpose and how to fulfill it. Funny enough, God had already told me what my purpose was at the age of twenty. A man of God told me I would be a speaker who would help people by sharing my story. Obviously, I ignored him because, at the time, that was not something

I was interested in. Moreover, what story was he talking about? I was only twenty. I had no story at the time!

I did enjoy doing my presentations in college; however, I didn't consider that a viable career choice or business venture. Also, the man of God made it seem as though I would be ministering in some way. I didn't want that! I did not think that I was qualified to minister to anyone. Truth is I didn't want the responsibility. At the time, I didn't know how to differentiate between being a minister at a church and ministering through my business or career.

Fast forward, I never forgot the conversation with the man of God; however, I did continue to run from it. I would pray constantly about my purpose while simultaneously evading it. I knew I had a passion for helping people. I also knew I had a passion for motivating and encouraging people through my words and actions. I would help people all the time by motivating and encouraging them. I would do research for them and find ways to help them succeed. Still, I looked at it as a hobby.

Helping people was just what I did. I didn't expect any payment for it. I just wanted to be of assistance in any way I could. I didn't feel this way while working as a claims adjuster. Actually, I wanted more money to do claims work. Investigating a claim for free? I think not!

While I was praying for my purpose, I started the nonprofit organization I spoke about in Chapter one. As you know, I discontinued that organization. My corporate job didn't work out for me, along with countless other business ideas I had. I couldn't figure out the reason why until I was honest with myself and became more confident in me and my abilities.

Finally, I put two and two together and realized that my purpose and passion were staring me in the face all along. I was meant to be a motivator and encourager.

So I ventured into being a coach and speaker. This has been the only consistent business for me thus far.

When you have a calling on your life, and you're operating in your purpose, you will know because it will stick. Of course, I had a little bit of help when the minister told me what my calling was ten years prior. However, I still had to go through my own process and take the necessary steps to realize it for myself.

Where are you in your journey right now? What qualities about yourself have you been ignoring? As my old pastor used to say: "The very thing you're looking for is right under your nose."

EXERCISE 3

At the back of the book, you will find the steps to get you closer to figuring out your passion. Complete that section and then return to this chapter.

Now, use those steps to figure out if you can make a decent living doing any of the things you listed. The online assessment results will help with this. You will need to think outside of the box. For example: if you love basketball, you could consider becoming a basketball coach for a middle school or starting a basketball camp for children/teens for a fee.

Research how you can make money living out your passion and purpose. A job title exists for the very thing you love to do. Once you know your passion, you will begin to understand your purpose. Your purpose is what you were placed on this earth to do. What will come from you achieving and living this passion? What legacy will you leave behind? You can live out your passion and

purpose at the same time.

Chapter 4

Step 4: Creating an Action Plan

Congratulations! You've made it to Step Four! At this point, you know what you're passionate about, how it relates to your purpose and how to monetize it with a business or career. The next step is creating an action plan. According to Dictionary.com, an action plan is a proposed strategy or course of action.

It is time to be strategic. You must put steps in place to live out your passion and purpose in a career or business. When we set goals, things don't always go as planned. However, having a documented plan in place to guide us along our journey is critical.

I know firsthand what it feels like when your plans don't work out as expected. When I started this business, I had everything lined up. I strategized how I was going to get my business off the ground. I would use my savings as startup capital and live with my brother and sister-in-law for a few months. That way, I could reduce my living expenses, work in my business full-time and eventually pay myself from the business so I could move out. Easy, right? Well, of course, life doesn't always go as planned, and I didn't think things through properly.

Firstly, I was unrealistic about how business and entrepreneurship worked. For most entrepreneurs, it takes time to make enough money after taxes and expenses to operate full-time. Also, I hadn't thoroughly researched my industry to find out what other coaches did to make enough profit to stand on their own. I really thought that once I made my business public, I would be flooded with clients. Boy, was I wrong.

Secondly, I didn't factor my personal life into my plan. I was in a long-distance relationship, and I was tired of driving six hours to see Ryan. I figured that since I was unemployed and no longer bound to a lease, I could move to Georgia and work on my business there. Well, it wasn't as easy as I thought it would be. I needed a part-time job to support myself while working on my business. I only had about six months of savings to live on.

Well, I applied and applied for part-time jobs with no luck. I even tried staffing agencies that specialized in insurance. Nope. Nothing. I prayed and had faith that God would provide for me. With peace in my spirit, I made the decision to move and use my savings to sustain me until I found a job. I found a roommate in my new city and packed my car to head to Georgia.

Once in Georgia, I applied for more part-time jobs and was rejected time after time. So I tried applying for full-time jobs. Yet again, I was rejected. Finally, I landed a part-time job at a restaurant and quit after three weeks. Terrible! I know. A couple of co-workers spoke to me in a crazy tone about straws and seating, so instead of showing them my behind, I walked out. I still had enough savings to get me through the next couple of months anyway.

A month later, I landed a job back in insurance claims and worked that for another two years. I had zero plans to return to insurance claims, but I had to do what I had to do to make ends meet. Also, during this time, I got engaged and married! As you can see, my original plan did not work at all. Life happened to me. However, my plan didn't work solely because life happens. Admittedly, I made mistakes with my initial action plan. I was unrealistic and did not do my research. Also, I didn't factor in my personal life. I created a plan based on emotion. I only thought about now, not later.

When creating your plan, do thorough research on your industry. Do you need to further your education with a degree or certificate? Do you need prior experience? What can you do to gain experience in the industry? Is there a certain area of the country you need to move to? Do you need a new wardrobe for interviews?

These are just a few of many questions you must ask yourself while creating your action plan.

The next thing you must factor in is your personal life. Do you have children to take care of? Do you have a spouse who may be affected by this goal? How will you factor your kids and spouse into your plan? Do you have the money in hand to achieve your goal? If not, do you know how you will get it? Have you set a budget? Most business ventures require startup capital. Without the funds to get going, you may need to put your plans on hold and try to raise the money. One way to do so is by working overtime or getting a second job.

I think by now you get the point that for your career or business to be successful, you must do in-depth planning and cover your bases. An action plan is not something you put together in 15 minutes. It takes time. As mentioned earlier you must:

a.   Research the industry

b. Factor in your personal life, which includes relationships and income.

c. Make sure you consider worst-case scenarios. Remember, life happens.

EXERCISE 4

I think you're ready now! Use the space at the back of the book to create your own plan.

Check out this sample action plan for a Fashion Design Major:

Ashley's Fearless Action Plan:

1. Research, Research, Research! - There are two routes you can potentially take:

    A.   Entrepreneurship: Personal Stylist

        1.   What do you need to do to become a personal stylist?
- Experience
- Build your Portfolio (of clients you've worked with or fashions you've put together)
- Existing clients (Goes with experience)
- Do some pro-bono styling to gain experience and build portfolio

    B.   Career: Fashion Merchandise Buyer

        1.   What does it take to become a Fashion Buyer?

- Fashion Degree (which you do have)
- Work in boutiques for experience
- Intern for a retailer or large boutique for experience

**Remember, you can work in a boutique while pursuing either endeavor. Be sure to stay in the field of fashion. You do not want to deviate from the line of work you want to go into. If you do, you may get stuck in a career you don't particularly care for.

2. Research the best cities for Fashion Buyers & Personal Stylists
   - Most likely, they will be larger cities
   - Start planning for relocation. Find friends or associates who may be interested in moving to the same area and become roommates. No Fear!
   - Research the cost of living & salaries in the area you're interested in

3. Write specific goals stating what you want in life...period. Be specific about your salary expectations and make sure it aligns with the market rate in that city. Think BIG. Set your 3 to 5 year goals.

4. Find a group, meet up or attend events to interact with other people in the fashion field/industry.

Chapter 5

Step 5: Taking Action

Yay, you've made it! Your action plan is complete. Now, you only have one step left to conquer; that is, taking action! It is time to act on the goals you have set. On the outside looking in, it seems as if it is an easy task to simply look at your plan and follow it. However, putting a plan in motion is easier said than done. It's simple to write down a goal but a lot harder to follow through and accomplish it. Honestly, I still struggle with taking the steps to accomplish the goals I have set.

Intentionally pursue the goals you have set for yourself. As an entrepreneur, you do not have anyone who will check-in with you every morning. You make your own schedule and hold yourself accountable for working on the goals you have set for your business and you. Accomplishing goals requires that you learn how to manage your time, do your research, and be motivated to reach those goals.

How are you spending your time during the day? Are you on social media instead of knocking out goal number one? If you want to achieve a goal in your action plan, you must make the time to do so. In fact, how you manage your time is crucial. It will determine whether you are successful or not. For example, if you need to get certified in a specific field or industry, you must incorporate study time into your day. Taking the steps to achieve your goals must become a part of your daily routine.

I understand we all have busy lives and squeezing in an ounce of time may seem impossible. If you struggle with finding time during your day to work on a goal, make some adjustments. Get up earlier in the morning or stay up a little later at night. There are 24 hours in a day. Use them wisely.

As I stated previously, researching and learning about the industry you are interested in takes time. However, it is a step in your action plan you must not ignore.

Let's say fitness is your passion, and you've understood how it relates to your purpose. You cannot jump into this without learning as much about it as possible. Why? Fitness is a broad industry with so many different elements and certifications. Also, several companies offer certifications for the fitness industry and others. Therefore, you need to find the best fit for you in terms of cost, location, what they offer, etc.

If you need to obtain a bachelors or master's degree for a specific career, be mindful that several colleges offer the same field of study, but you must ensure you do your research on the accreditation and costs. Online resources are also available to help you narrow down the best choices for your specific industry. Take the time needed to investigate and establish the best place to obtain your certifications, licenses or degrees. Even if your industry of choice doesn't require a degree or certification, do your research.

As a coach, I had to take a course to learn more about the industry, how to structure my business, coaching styles, etc. It would be nice to figure out your passion and purpose then get to work right away but that doesn't always end well.

You may already have experience in a particular industry and want to start your own business. You must still do adequate research on how to run a business. Entrepreneurship is not only about the knowledge of an industry, but it also involves networking, time-management, and budgeting. You also need to understand the market trends and how to use technology to your advantage.

Lastly, you must be motivated to achieve the goal. What motivates you to get out of bed every day? Remember your *why*. Why do you want to live a life of purpose? Who will benefit from you living out your purpose through your career or business? In order to reach your goals, you must remember your *why* every single day. You have made it to this last step for a reason. Every time you feel discouraged just remember your *why*.

Your *why* doesn't have to make sense to anyone but you. I have multiple "whys." I want to be my own boss, make my own rules, and set my own schedules. I also want the freedom to work from anywhere. Who wouldn't want to work sitting on the white sands of the Bahamas with a tropical drink by your side? I'll wait.

I also want to leave a legacy of hard work, dedication, perseverance, and outrageous giving. I want to leave an inheritance for my future children. Last but certainly not least, I want to serve the Lord and His people. I know I was placed on this earth to be greater than myself. My purpose is to help and give back to others what God has given me.

Hiring a coach to motivate you and hold you accountable helps greatly as well. If you can't afford an expert coach, a friend, family member or spouse can become your accountability partner. Whatever you need to do to stay motivated, do it. Even though I am naturally a go-getter and motivated person, I still need an extra push from my loved ones.

We are all human and at times, we won't feel like working on our goals. However, don't stay in those moments too long. Someone is counting on you to walk in your purpose; don't let that person or yourself down. I believe God orders our steps in every way. However, we must put in the work to achieve what He has for us.

"In the same way, faith by itself, if it is not accompanied by action, is dead" - James 2:17

Praying, fasting and having faith alone will not get you your heart's desires. Once you hear from the Lord, you must do the work. We all have choices in life. God cannot make us do anything we do not want to do.

At times in my life, I was so down that working on my passion and purpose was the furthest thing from my mind. However, in those low periods, I had to make the decision to just do it! As much as I wanted to be selfish, I knew other people were counting on me to motivate and encourage them.

So many people private message me telling me how I have helped them through a post on social media. Wow! Others have also told me I have encouraged and inspired them by the way I live my life. How can I give up? Giving up isn't an option for me. I can't let anyone down. I can't let myself down and most importantly, I can't let God down.

You must decide every single day that you are going to get out of bed and work on your purpose. You must be able to manage your time wisely, do your research, and stay motivated.

Chapter 6

Having Support

Have you ever experienced a major event in your life when your friends or family were there to help you? If so, their help came in handy, right? Absolutely! Having the support of family, friends, associates and even online groups makes pursuing your purpose much more fulfilling.

You will be satisfied once you're living in your purpose. However, in your pursuit, you may become discouraged or overwhelmed. In these moments, having a shoulder to lean on can make all the difference. It will encourage and motivate you. Support from family, friends or associates fuels you to keep going because you know you're not on this journey alone.

I hear a lot of people say they want to keep their "moves" private so no one steals their ideas or "hates" on them. I totally understand that way of thinking, and I agree to a certain extent. I agree to not tell your 2,000 followers on social media every goal you're working toward.

I also agree that you must use discernment when confiding in people about your goals. However, discussing these matters with friends, associates or family you trust is necessary. Life has its ups and downs and in those down moments, it's nice to turn to someone for extra confidence or motivation. Also, you never know what contacts a friend or family member may have that can help you.

I used to keep everything to myself, including business ideas. All that did was stress me out more because I had no one to talk to. Being able to vent about your journey helps, even if you don't need the person to say anything. Just letting out your frustrations can assist in relieving some stress during your endeavor. I know what it is like not to have the support you need while pursuing a major goal in your life. It's hard. I also know what it's like to have support. It feels good.

The support of my husband, close friends, and family helped me tremendously. Even if the only shoulder I had to lean on was my husband's, that would have been enough for me. Everyone will not stand by you in difficult times. In fact, some people will be jealous if they know what you're working toward. Lean on the people you trust and who sincerely support you. Remember to show appreciation.

Always focus on the positive instead of the negative while on your journey. Too often, we tend to concentrate on the people who don't support rather than the ones who are there for us.

If you do not have close family or friends, join a local or online organization or group. There may even be anonymous groups you can connect with if that makes you feel better. You don't need to get into an in-depth conversation about your idea or goals; however, talking to people who are on a similar journey as you helps a lot. Some people even make friends after joining such groups or organizations. You never know what can happen so instead of being so secretive about your goals, share and enjoy the journey.

Another way to have support while pursuing your purpose is to find a mentor in your industry. You can find mentors in local organizations, at networking events, and even on social media. Don't be afraid to reach out to someone who has experience in your line of work. Send the person a message or email; alternatively, you can approach him or her at a networking event. Shoot your shot!

Several people out there would love to help and mentor the next generation. If you reach out to a couple of people, but they do not respond, find others. Don't allow rejection to prevent you from getting the help you need to be the best you can be. A mentor will guide you along your journey by encouraging you, giving tips on the industry and providing hands-on training or shadowing in that field. Some of the most successful people have had mentors to help and guide them along the way.

With all of the support that's available in so many ways, don't forget the *One* who supports you the most. The Lord is always there for you.

As you're going through your journey, God's Word is also available to encourage you. Remember you are never alone. "So do not fear, for I am with you; do not be dismayed, for I am your God; I will strengthen you and help you; I will uphold you with my righteous right hand" (Isaiah 41:10).

At the end of the day, having support from one person or multiple people will help you tremendously on your journey to fulfilling your passion and purpose. Again, you are not on this journey alone. So many people are rooting for you and want to help. Let them in. I promise you won't regret it.

Chapter 7

Perseverance

Perseverance is persistence in doing something despite difficulty or delay in achieving success (Dictionary.com). Have you ever had your mind set on a goal that was more difficult or took longer to reach than you expected? Did you give up because it was hard or took too long? Or did you stick with it until you got it?

The goal could be joining a sports team at school, joining a fraternity or sorority, learning an instrument or moving to the city you've always dreamed of. Didn't it feel good once you finally reached the goal you set for yourself? Aren't you glad you didn't give up and turn away because it was too hard or took too long?

I have to raise my hand because I wanted to give up so many times on my journey to fulfilling my purpose in life. I am so happy I didn't give up or give in to fear. If I had given up on my purpose, I would not have been able to help you and countless others who are relying on me. I would let myself down and most importantly, God, who gave me this purpose to help others find their way in their careers and businesses. Who is counting on you to fulfill your purpose? By now, you understand that your purpose is bigger than you. You want to make an impact in this world, and you will as long as you stay the course.

While pursuing your passion and purpose, you will be faced with obstacles to overcome such as fear, life changes, and rejection, to name a few. I have had to overcome all three of those obstacles my entire life. I feared what other people thought of me. I have gone through many life changes: jobs, moving to a different state, marriage, overcoming anxiety and depression, etc.

I've also been rejected and ignored while pursuing my passion and purpose. I've reached out to multiple people for help with no responses. I've also pitched my business with no luck at all. I know how it feels to want something so badly you can taste it and try to achieve a goal that seems unreachable.

On the flip side, I know how it feels when I do get that call back. I know how it feels to be stable and secure in my life. I also know how it feels to finally get that "yes" after so many no's. Now, let's dig into how to overcome fear, life changes, and rejection.

Fear: False Evidence Appearing Real. Have you ever seen that acronym for fear? The true definition of fear is an unpleasant emotion caused by the belief that someone or something is dangerous, likely to cause pain or a threat (Dictionary.com). Have you experienced fear in your life in any area? Isn't it paralyzing at times? Fear can literally stop you in your tracks and prevent you from doing something you set out to do.

Some people have a fear of public speaking; therefore, they will turn down speaking engagements and other opportunities that showcase their expertise. People are willing to lose out on amazing opportunities and money because of fear. I can relate because I was like that. I worried about people not liking me for whatever reason. What if I mess up the speech I've rehearsed countless times? What if I don't make any sense in my online posts or even with this book? Well, guess what? There is no need to fear. God has not given us the spirit of fear but of power, love, and of a sound mind (2 Timothy 1:7). You are pursuing your purpose for God, not man. And you know what? God has already validated you and made you the expert because *He* called you for this purpose.

You are pursuing this purpose for God and you, not to please the masses. The people you are supposed to reach will understand what you're doing and will receive it well. Cast your cares on the Lord, and He will sustain you. He will never let the righteous be shaken (Psalms 55:22).

Now that we've tackled fear, what about those life changes I mentioned? How do you persevere through life's circumstances? Have you ever had to make unexpected changes to your life? Making adjustments may mean delaying something you were working on, like going to school or starting a business. For instance, when I incorporated my business in 2016, I made the decision to move to Atlanta, GA to be closer to Ryan.

After making that move, I couldn't focus on my business as much because I needed a job to pay my bills. Also, I got engaged a year later. Shortly after Ryan and I got married, I was diagnosed with depression and anxiety because I was so stressed and overwhelmed with work. I was also extremely homesick, and I felt as if I didn't have the support I needed outside of my husband who was working a job with late hours. I was very lonely.

Many things happened to take my focus off my business. Actually, I didn't launch it until the summer of 2018. Yet, I didn't allow all the changes I went through to keep me down. I pressed on and pursued my purpose. I knew I couldn't allow anything to make me give up, even if it took longer to achieve.

If major life changes happen as you're pursuing your purpose, take the time you need to readjust. Life is going to happen, just don't allow the changes and circumstances to stop your journey completely. As the Bible says, "I press on toward the goal to win the prize for which God has called me heavenward in Christ Jesus" (Philippians 3:14).

Lastly, I want to briefly touch on persevering through rejection. When I moved to Atlanta, I felt as if I couldn't find a job to save my life! I applied and interviewed at several places with no luck. I received rejection emails galore.

I remember one evening, a rejection email came to my inbox and all I could do was cry. Not again. Why didn't they want me? Did I say something wrong in the interview? Did I make a mistake moving to Atlanta? So many thoughts ran through my head. I felt defeated. I was on the brink of moving back home to NC. After receiving encouragement from Ryan, I decided to stick it out.

Not long after, I received a job offer that got me back on my feet. If I had given up and moved back to NC because of rejection, I may not have gotten married a year later. I may not have had the drive to continue my business or write this book. Who knows?

I do know rejection made me stronger as a career woman, wife, and businesswoman. Rejection is going to occur while you're pursuing and living out your purpose; it is just part of the course. Therefore, keep striving toward your purpose no matter what!

"Stand firm, and you will win life." - Luke 21:19

Conclusion

You have made it to the end of the book; however, your journey is just beginning. You are about to embark on an amazing and exciting journey to find and fulfill your passion and purpose. Get ready to enjoy a fulfilling life as you operate in your purpose.

Living a life of purpose is rare in a world full of people who are just working to make ends meet. Operating in your purpose guarantees a life filled with happiness and joy. You'll have days that are harder than others because that's life; we can't control everything that happens. However, we can control how we deal with life's circumstances and the paths we decide to take.

You can do this! God put you on this earth for a reason —to fulfill your purpose in life.

EXERCISE 1

1. What are your motives for pursuing a career or business?

   What are you seeking out of a career or business?

   _____

   _____

   _____

   _____

   _____

   _____

   _____

   _____

   _____

   _____

   _____

   _____

2. Are you driven by money or passion and purpose?

   Explain why.

   _____

   _____

   _____

   _____

   _____

   _____

   _____

   _____

   _____

   _____

   _____

   _____

   _____

3. What kind of life do you want to live? Explain.

_____

_____

_____

_____

_____

_____

_____

_____

_____

_____

_____

_____

_____

4. What do success and your dream life look like to you?

_____

_____

_____

_____

_____

_____

_____

_____

_____

_____

_____

_____

_____

EXERCISE 2

1. List at least 7 to 10 overall good qualities about yourself.

   There are great things about you!

   _____

   _____

   _____

   _____

   _____

   _____

   _____

   _____

   _____

   _____

   _____

2. List the good qualities you possess in the workplace or

   school (current or past).

_____

_____

_____

_____

_____

_____

_____

_____

_____

_____

_____

_____

3. Survey close friends, family, co-workers or classmates about the good qualities you possess. Write them down below:

---

4. Practice! Practice your craft repeatedly until you feel confident about it. Each time, you will get better and feel better about it. Use this section to write what makes you a great fit for this line of work.

_____

_____

_____

_____

_____

_____

_____

_____

_____

_____

_____

_____

_____

_____

EXERCISE 3

1. List your likes/dislikes in a career or business (this is for

    any job). What kind of work environment do you

    like/dislike?

    _____

    _____

    _____

    _____

    _____

    _____

    _____

    _____

    _____

2. List the top 3 things you love to do/hobbies (Things you would do every day without getting paid.)

_____

_____

_____

_____

_____

_____

_____

_____

_____

_____

_____

_____

3. Go online and search for free career self-assessment tests. I like the human metrics exam. The end of the exam will have a list of industries that best match your personality per the test. Choose three to five careers/industries that most interest you. Do your research on them to see what they're about if you don't know. Write them below.

_____

_____

_____

_____

_____

_____

_____

_____

_____

_____

4. "Your Perfect Day" exercise: Describe your perfect day.

   Make sure you are very specific and think outside of the

   box. This should represent what a day in your life would

   be like if you had unlimited resources and no time

   constraints.

———————————————————————

———————————————————————

———————————————————————

———————————————————————

———————————————————————

———————————————————————

———————————————————————

———————————————————————

———————————————————————

———————————————————————

———————————————————————

EXERCISE 4

Example Goals for Your Action Plan

Entrepreneurship Goals
- Write a business plan
- File articles of incorporation
- Apply for an EIN
- Open business account
- Hire a graphic designer or design website, logo, and business cards
- Put together a marketing and advertisement plan to get clients
- Update social media pages
- Attend networking events to connect with other entrepreneurs and seek clients

Career Goals
- Update resume and LinkedIn to broaden skills and make yourself more marketable to future employers
- Obtain certifications or degree required for the type of career you are interested in
- Participate in mock interview sessions with a coach or friend in the field of work you are interested in
- Participate in webinars and other training to acquire more information about a particular career
- Find a mentor in the field you are interested in and explore possible shadowing opportunities

Action Plan Tip #2

When you create your plan, don't forget one of the most important factors to getting you one step closer to your dreams: money! Think about the following while you create your own plan:

- Can you afford this?
- Are you in a position to take a pay cut if necessary?
- Bills vs. new job (be smart!)
- Who will it affect?

A Few Examples of What Costs You Will Incur
- Hiring a resume writer
- New clothes for interview, hair, manicures (looking your best is a big part of getting a job!)
- Cost of going back to school for a degree or certification (apply for scholarships and grants)
- Hiring a career coach
- Costs associated with incorporating a business: Average cost is $200 for filing articles of incorporation (varies with state)

Startup Costs Depending on Type of Business
- Websites (there are free website themes; however, you do have to pay for the hosting and domain)
- Business cards, logos, brochures (VistaPrint and other sites offer low-cost options)
- Photoshoots (a low-cost option is to use your cell phone to start)
- Equipment (computers and anything else needed for your specific business)
- Business Coach/Consultant
- Finding a location to buy or lease (Some startups can be done out of your home

Use the spaces below to write your action plan. Refer to Chapter 4 for help.

_____

_____

_____

_____

_____

_____

_____

_____

_____

_____

_____

_____

_____

THE PURPOSED JOURNEY

_____

_____

_____

_____

_____

_____

_____

_____

_____

_____

_____

_____

_____

_____

_____

www.ingramcontent.com/pod-product-compliance
Lightning Source LLC
Chambersburg PA
CBHW051737040426
42447CB00008B/1173